BYOU ARE MY ELOVED

Meditations on God's Steadfast Love

MITCH FINLEY

Resurrection Press
Mineola • New York

Dedication

For the monks of Our Lady of Guadalupe
Trappist Abbey, Lafayette, Oregon.

In memory of
Father Bernard McVeigh, o.c.s.o. (1918-1997),
Abbot of Guadalupe 1974-1994.

O give thanks to the LORD, for he is good;
for his steadfast love endures forever
(1 Chronicles 16:34).

First published in 1999 by Resurrection Press, Ltd.
P.O. Box 248
Williston Park, NY 11596

Copyright © 1999 by Mitch Finley

ISBN 1-878718-49-5
Library of Congress Catalog Card Number 98-68008

All Bible quotations are from the New Revised Standard Version Bible: Catholic Edition, Copyright 1989, 1993, Division of Christian Education of the National Council of the Churches of Christ in the United States of America.

Cover design by John Murello

Printed in the United States of America.

Contents

Foreword

I've known Mitch Finley for many years. When I was asked if I would write a few words for this book, I was delighted because, in his writings — and in his life — Mitch celebrates the profound love God has for each of us. The deep intricacies of theology, the modern equivalents of "how many angels can dance on the head of a pin," the factions, the fractions and the future, Mitch blessedly leaves to others. He does what he does best — bring the message of God's love into the lives of everyday people.

He does so by using the alchemy of Faith to turn the events of daily living into a manifestation of thanksgiving and grace. Of all the things I appreciate about Mitch's writing, perhaps the greatest is his ability to put the message of the Gospels into ordinary, everyday language. In his hands, it is indeed, "good news."

This book is no exception. Throughout its pages, Mitch takes each of us by the hand, and like a patient teacher, shows us over and over how much God loves us; how much God cares for us; how important we are to God. Along with G.K. Chesterton he points out that our relationship with God is not a theory, but a "love affair."

A love affair with God, and I might add, with the Church, is an appropriate image for Mitch. Mitch loves being a Catholic. He may not always love everything or everyone in the Church, but his love for his Faith is obvious to all who know him. Time and again, he has reminded me in his words and his writings that God did not become a human to bring suffering and sorrow to the world. God did not establish a Church to burden us with increasingly heavy rules and regulations. God became human out of love. God established a Church to help us live in love. Mitch is thoroughly, wonderfully, joyfully Catholic...and his writings make us glad that we share a symbolic pew in the same Church.

There are so many wonderful reflections in this book, I would be hard pressed to pick a favorite, but one that particularly affected me contains the lines, "We are so inclined to believe that God will stop loving us for the slightest reason, at the drop of a hat. We are so inclined to believe that when pain, or grief, or hard times come to us that must mean that God does not love me." (I'm not going to tell you where the quote comes from. You'll just have to read the book and discover for yourself!) Many times, in my life, I've felt just that way. I've doubted God's love because I could barely love myself. Mitch reminds me that my feelings have nothing to do with God's love, which is steadfast, eternal and always available.

I hope you will take the time to meditate on these reflections; to let their message seep deep into the arid spots in your soul; to let their insights water and nourish your relationship with God who loves you as if you were the only person on earth. I have, and once again I have been blessed by Mitch's words — and the reality of God's love.

WOODEENE KOENIG-BRICKER,
author of *365 Mary*

Introduction

God loves you with a passionate, never-ending, unconditional love. That means you, gentle reader, and it means everyone you know; it means me, the author of this book, and it means each and every person in the world. No strings attached. No red tape. No small print. God loves you with a love that is beyond measure; God loves you more than you can imagine or hope for. That is why, in the Gospels, Jesus bends over backward telling people to stop being anxious or afraid. If God loves you, the ideal is to not let fear or anxiety control your life.

This message is simple yet profound, and it is a message of joy. This news about God's love for you is so good, in fact, that much of the time you may find it difficult to believe. You may believe that God loves you in theory, but to accept that God loves you, you there with your face hanging out — well, that can be tough. Much of the time, in fact, we act as if God not only does not love us but is indifferent towards us.

Someone once asked the great theologian Karl Rahner to summarize all of his vast theological reflections in one short sentence. Rahner thought for a moment, then replied: "God lives in you." That is the heart of the message, that God loves you so much that God lives in you — and you live in God. This is the heart and soul of the matter, that you live in God, and God lives in you, and God is love.

St. Augustine of Hippo said some fifteen hundred years ago that God is closer to you than you are to yourself. Because God is love, this means that love, God's love, is closer to you than you are to yourself. It is impossible to carry this to extremes; it is impossible to state this too strongly. God is love, and God loves you with a love that surrounds and penetrates you at all times and in all places. God's love is the air you breathe; God's love is the food you eat; and God's love for you is absolutely reliable. There is nothing necessarily Christian, even, about this truth. St. Paul, in the Acts of the Apostles, quotes with approval ancient Greek philosophers: "For 'In him we live and move and have our being'; as even some of your own poets have said . . ." (Acts 17:28).

It is the purpose of this small book to serve as a resource to remind yourself of God's unconditional, steadfast love. Just about every day we need to remind ourselves of the depth of God's love for us, so each of the reflections in this book serves as a daily reminder. This book's purpose will be accomplished particularly well if each reflection leads you to a moment of prayer, a moment to bask in an awareness of God's never-ending love for you.

Book 1

I am not worthy of the least of all the steadfast love
and all the faithfulness that you have shown to your
servant. . .   (GENESIS 32:10)

Someone reminds you that God loves you.
Fear not, friend, God loves you.
You nod your head in agreement.
But in the back of your mind a little voice
        whispers:
"You are not worthy of God's love. Not you."
You feel unworthy of God's love,
and so you do not truly believe
that God loves you.
For you are not worthy of God's love.
"I am a bad person in so many ways."
Which is true: you are a stinker.
You are frequently unloving, insensitive,
and mean to other people.
You frequently act with no faith.
Maybe you have an addiction or two,
and that makes you unworthy of God's love.
So we are agreed.
You are not worthy of God's love.
There it is, on the table for all to see.
You are not worthy of God's love.

Have I got news for you.
Don't feel like the Lone Ranger.
Nobody is worthy of God's love.
Not you, not me, not anybody.
But that, my friend, is irrelevant.
God loves you in spite of all your faults and
    failings.
God loves you even though you are not worthy.
Worthy, smurthy, God says,
I love you madly, every atom of your being.
So there.
I love you anyway.
Stick that in your backpack and take a hike with
    it.
Let us have no more talk of worthy and unworthy.
God loves you endlessly, unconditionally,
and God, who is love, lives in you all the livelong
    day.
Worthy, smurthy.
God loves you anyway.

*In your steadfast love you led the people whom you
redeemed; you guided them by your strength to your
holy abode.* (EXODUS 15:13)

God's love for you is "steadfast."
This phrase, "steadfast love," occurs time after
    time
in the Hebrew Scriptures, the Old Testament.
You think you can count on a mountain
to stay where it is?
God's love is far more reliable.
You think the stars will stay where they are
in the night sky, utterly predictable
as they seem to dance around the moon?
God's love for you is far more predictable.
You think you can trust that the sun
will rise in the morning,
and set in the evening?
God's loving presence in you
is more trustworthy than that.

Here is what God's steadfast love is like:
Recall the painting on the ceiling of the Sistine
    Chapel in Rome, by Michaelangelo.

There you see God portrayed as an old man,
with a flowing grey beard,
his arm and forefinger extended toward Adam
in the act of creation.
God is an old man with a long grey beard.
That is one way to say that God's love is reliable.
As we may trust a good old man,
so we may trust in God's love for us.
This is a metaphor, to view God as an old man,
and when it comes to God
all we have are metaphors and analogies.
But look at another metaphor.
God is young, young as spring, and ever new.
See God's love in the exuberance of youth,
see God's love in the readiness of young people
to drop everything and rush off to serve others
at a moment's notice.
God's steadfast love is like this,
always ready at a moment's notice.

But while he was still far off, his father saw him and was filled with compassion; he ran and put his arms around him and kissed him. (LUKE 15:20B)

The story traditionally called
"The Parable of the Prodigal Son"
is a story of forgiveness.
Sometimes, however, we miss
the bigger picture.
Why does the father forgive his son?
The father forgives his son because
he loves him.
The father does not say, "What have you been up
to?"
or "You should be ashamed of yourself."
Instead, as soon as he sees who it is,
the father's heart fills with love.
He runs, and runs, and runs,
and he throws his arms around his son
and kisses him.

Jesus tells this story to wake us up,
to give us a hint.
Jesus tells this story so we

will not be clueless
when it comes to God's love for us.
No matter what we have done,
no matter how we have lived our life,
as long as we are sorry,
God our loving Father
runs, and runs, and runs to meet us,
holds us in an embrace, a good long hug,
like the father of the prodigal son,
only more so.
That, Jesus says, is what God's love for us is like.
At least it's a hint, a general idea,
so that we will not be clueless about God's love.

O give thanks to the Lord, for he is good; his steadfast love endures forever! (Psalm 118:1)

We have such a difficult time remembering
that God's love "endures forever."
We say we believe it, of course.
But when we have troubles,
when things go wrong,
when people we love make
self-destructive choices,
choices that hurt us, as well,
then we have a difficult time believing in
God's love for us.
Then we have a difficult time believing in
God's love for the other person.
We beg God to do this and that;
we give Him detailed instructions:
Dear God, we pray, "Make her do this,"
or "Make him stop doing that."

If we believe in God's love, however,
we need to pray, instead, like this:
"Help me to trust in your steadfast love,
your steadfast love for him,

your steadfast love for her,
your steadfast love for me.
Help me to trust that you will take care of
what needs to be taken care of.
May your will be done in his life.
May your will be done in her life.
May your will be done in my life."
This is what it means to trust in God's love.
More and more we need to give ourselves to this
prayer of love,
this prayer of trust in God's love.

". . .for the Father himself loves you, because you have loved me and have believed that I came from God." (JOHN 16:27)

God your loving Father, "loving Papa"
— which is what *Abba* really means —
loves you even more than the most loving Father
ever loved his child.
Even more than that.
God your loving Father loves you passionately,
mindlessly, blindly,
couldn't care less about your faults and failings,
your petty little sins, even your big sins.
Why does God love you so completely?
Is it because you are a blooming saint?
Not likely.
Is it because you are a perfect person?
Probably not.

God loves you because you are you,
absolutely unique, absolutely special.
God loves you
because you love His Son,
who is the risen Lord,

and you believe that he came from the Father.
Not saying you have a perfect faith,
never have any doubts or questions.
Saying that in your best moments
you do believe.
Therefore, God loves you deeply, endlessly
in your best moments
and in your not-so-great moments.
God loves you always and everywhere.
God loves you from the top of your head
to the tips of your toes.

You shall love the LORD your God with all your heart, and with all your soul, and with all your might. (DEUTERONOMY 6:5)

We have heard these words
so many times.
We nod agreeably.
Yes, yes, this is a great commandment.
But secretly we wonder
how on earth a person is supposed to
love God?
God is invisible, after all.
God seems to be everywhere
and nowhere.
So how does a person love God,
for heaven's sake?

You love God the same way you
love a human being.
You love God by making time
to be with God.
You love God by
paying attention to God,
by allowing God to give Himself to you,

and by giving yourself to God.
You love God the same way you
love anyone you love
only more so.
Of course, it helps if first
you feel loved by God,
and the best way to feel God's love is to
be quiet and tell God that
you want to feel His love.
And you will, you will.
You will feel God's love and want to
love God in return.

So now, O Israel, what does the LORD your God
require of you? Only to fear the LORD your God, to
walk in all his ways, to love him, to serve the LORD
your God with all your heart and with all your soul,
and to keep the commandments of the LORD your
God and his decrees. . .for your own well-being.

(DEUTERONOMY 10:12-13)

Astounding, mind boggling as it may seem,
our God wants our love.
Everybody wants to be loved
. . .even God!
The infinite, all-loving God
wants the love of His finite, human creatures.
If you can imagine.
God wants your love.
But what's all this talk about
commandments?
Funny thing about commandments.
All they are is love in action,
love in a practical form.

Take a look at the Ten Commandments
again sometime.

What you see are guidelines,
tips on a lifestyle based on practical,
non-romantic, no-nonsense love.
Not only that,
but the Ten Commandments
are for our own well-being!
If you know what's good for you,
God says,
you will follow my commandments.
If you want a life worth living,
with a minimum of grief caused by yourself,
you will follow my commandments.
It's as simple as that.

For I am convinced that neither death, nor life, nor
angels, nor rulers, nor things present, nor things to
come, nor powers, nor height, nor depth, nor
anything else in all creation, will be able to separate
us from the love of God in Christ Jesus our Lord.

(ROMANS 8:38-39)

We have the habit, sometimes,
of thinking that there is
a Great Distance between us and God.
God *waaay* up there,
us *waaay* down here.
Phooey, says St. Paul.
Get a grip.
There is nothing, nothing, nothing
that can separate us from God's love.
Nothing and no one.
Not life, certainly not death, and most definitely
    not
anything that you think might happen.
Most definitely not.
Sometimes we find it so difficult
to believe this,

that God's love is in me, and all around me
all of the time, everywhere, no matter what.
No question,
it can be difficult to believe this.
But there is a solution to this problem.

Listen up.
Act as if it is true that God's love
permeates your whole being.
Live your day as if it is true.
Make believe.
Then, to your delight and wonder,
you will discover that it is true!
You and God, you are like that:
closer than two peas in a pod.

"In your steadfast love you led the people whom you redeemed; you guided them by your strength to your holy abode." (EXODUS 15:13)

God led His people, Israel,
through the desert for forty years
to the Promised Land.
And why did God do this?
Because of His "steadfast love."
It's the old, old story of steadfast love.
But wait.
Here is an amazing, amazing,
amazing thing:
God leads each of us,
in His steadfast love,
through our own personal pilgrimage,
to His "holy abode."
When we feel lost,
when we wonder where we are,
and what is coming next,
it is time to remember that
God is leading us
in His steadfast love.
No matter how difficult

your life may become,
no matter how much anguish
you may experience,
God's steadfast love is all around
and within you.

Sit down, breathe deeply, and
remember this.
Entrust yourself once again
to God's steadfast love.
God's love is all around you;
God's love permeates every atom of your being.

And [Jesus] said to them, "Why are you afraid, you of little faith?" (MATTHEW 8:26)

If the message of Jesus,
and his purpose in coming into the world
can be summarized in just a few words
it would go something like this:
God loves you endlessly,
His love is like the love of a loving Papa
for his children.
Therefore, you need not be afraid,
not now, not ever.
You do not need to be afraid of
what might happen.
If you are afraid, Jesus says,
that means you have "little faith."

Why should faith result in
not being afraid?
Think of a warm, loving friendship.
You know you can trust your friend
unconditionally.
You know that he or she will
care for you,

no matter what.
Faith is like this.
Faith, at rock bottom,
is loving intimacy with God.
Only in this case we can trust that God
will be faithful to the end.
No matter how much anguish we may know
in this life, ultimately,
we can trust in God's love.
We need not be afraid.

Love is patient; love is kind. . . . It bears all things,
believes all things, hopes all things, endures all
things. Love never ends. (1 CORINTHIANS 13:4-8)

Typically, when we read or hear
St. Paul's famous ode to love
in First Corinthians Thirteen,
we take it as a reminder
of how we should act
if we would act with love.
Appropriately so.
But another perspective is also possible.
The First Letter of John declares that,
"God is love."
Holy guacamole!
Read First Corinthians Thirteen again,
but this time each time St. Paul says "love"
substitute "God."
Holy guacamole again!
We learn amazing things about God
and about His love for us,
what God's love is like!

God is patient;
God is kind;
God is not irritable
or resentful.
God bears all things,
believes all things,
hopes all things,
endures all things.
Holy guacamole!
This is how God is with us.
This is how God our Father loves.
This is how God loves you!

And do not keep striving for what you are to eat and what you are to drink, and do not keep worrying. For it is the nations of the world that strive after all these things, and your Father knows that you need them. (LUKE 12:29-30)

We knock ourselves out
trying to become as secure as possible.
Wouldn't we just love to win
a lottery?
A few million clams?
Talk to someone who is wealthy, however,
and you will discover that even wealth
does not guarantee emotional security
and peace of mind.
No way,
no how.
People who are wealthy
are just as inclined to be
anxious and afraid
as people who are not wealthy.
They may not worry about
paying the bills,
but they worry about

their children,
and they worry about
their marriages,
and sometimes they worry about
possibly losing their wealth.

Wealthy or otherwise,
Jesus tells us to
stop worrying because
in the long run
the only reliable peace of mind
comes from trust in God's love.

Is Ephraim my dear son? Is he the child I delight in?
As often as I speak against him, I still remember
him. Therefore I am deeply moved for him; I will
surely have mercy on him, says the LORD.
(JEREMIAH 31:20)

Your parents, most likely,
did not name you Ephraim.
But for now either think of yourself
as Ephraim,
or insert your own name in place of "Ephraim"
in the quotation above.
God says that you are His "dear son."
If you are female, of course, God says that you are
     His "dear daughter."

Yes, you. You there with your ordinary face
hanging out,
you are the child God "delights in."
As often as you frustrate the daylights
out of God your loving Father,
He still remembers you,
would never forget you.

When God thinks of you
— which is constantly
— He is "deeply moved" by the very thought.
This is truer than
the day is long.
You have made more than your share of
stupid choices.
You regularly act in
selfish, self-centered ways.
You sinner, you.
Hey. It's water under the bridge,
spilt milk it's no use crying over.
God "will surely have mercy" on you.
Absolutely, positively, no question about it.

See what love the Father has given us, that we should be called children of God; and that is what we are.   (1 JOHN 3:1)

Metaphors and analogies,
all we have to talk about God
and our experience of God
(which is what faith is)
are metaphors and analogies.
Thing is,
when it comes to the metaphors and analogies
of Christianity,
they not only limp,
they stagger about a good deal, too.
We are God's children.
That's a metaphor,
and it is all we have to express
a wonderful truth.
But this metaphor,
wonderful as it is,
needs to be magnified a hundred times
or more.

See what love God our Father gives us.

This is so true that we are God's own children.
The point is to give us a hint
about how deep God's love is for us.
God loves you so much,
so overwhelmingly,
that He is,
in fact, not by way of analogy,
your loving Father, loving Papa.
You are God's own child,
and His love covers you
like a warm patchwork quilt
on a cold winter night.

I am my beloved's, and his desire is for me.

(SONG OF SOLOMON 7:10)

There are different ways to read
the Song of Solomon.
Clearly, it was first written
as an erotic love poem
about the love between
a young man and a young woman.
Yet here it is in the Bible,
included among all the other
divinely inspired books.
The Song of Solomon reminds us
of the goodness of erotic love.
But for centuries the Song of Solomon
has also been interpreted to illustrate
the loving intimacy between God and us.
God is the groom and we are the bride.
Throughout the Song of Solomon
we learn not only that God loves us.
We learn that God loves us
like a passionately aroused lover
loves the young woman he is in love with.

Is it a scandal
that the Bible would use erotic love
to teach us about God's love for us?
No way.
It is good for us to know
that God's love for us
is "blind,"
that just as an aroused lover
disregards his lover's imperfections,
so God overlooks your sinfulness
because He is so madly, passionately
in love with you.

"For God so loved the world that he gave his only Son, so that everyone who believes in him may not perish but may have eternal life." (JOHN 3:16)

*I*t's astonishing, sometimes,
to realize how deep God's love is
for each and every one of us.
God loves,
and that is all that God does.
God loves you,
and that's all that God does.
And what do you need to do?
Very little,
almost nothing,
which turns out to be
everything.
All you need to do is
"believe in him."

*D*oes this mean you must merely
acknowledge, intellectually, that Christ is
who he says he is?
That, but much more than that.
To believe in Christ is, above all,

to trust in him.
But this is not so difficult
because God loves you
so much, so deeply, so unconditionally,
that to trust in His Son is
all you need to do.
Oh, it is a struggle sometimes,
we all know that.
But what matters is not trusting
perfectly all the time,
but beginning to trust again each day.
That's the way.

Be very careful. . .to love the LORD your God.

(JOSHUA 23:11)

God your loving Father loves you
so much,
so immeasurably much,
and all God asks is that
you love Him in return.
God your loving Father wants nothing less
than your heart.
Does this seem like too much of an
abstraction?
Do you wonder how anyone can
love God,
who is so beyond anything we can
say or think about Him?

No problem.
Let us not lose sight of
one of the main reasons Jesus came,
to teach us that God is not an abstraction.
Rather, God is our loving Father,
and that is how we are to think of God.
When we do this,

we should have no trouble loving God.
"Be very careful," says Joshua,
". . .to love the LORD your God."
Be very careful.
That is such a gentle way to say it.
Be very careful to love God your loving Father.
Be very careful to love Him, and
that does not mean trembling with terror
in God's presence.
It means climbing into His lap,
as a child snuggles into a loving Father's lap.

[Solomon] said, "O LORD, God of Israel, there is no God like you in heaven above or on earth beneath, keeping covenant and steadfast love for your servants who walk before you with all their heart. . ." (1 KINGS 8:23)

God is our loving Father,
but His love is far better than that
of any human father.
No matter how good a human father may be
there are times when he is
in a bad mood,
or tired,
or unavailable.
A human father's love
is never completely perfect.
God's love,
on the other hand,
is "steadfast,"
completely reliable,
always there,
always trustworthy.
God does not get tired
of loving you.

Our love is imperfect, of course,
and our love is sometimes weak.
Our love is sometimes unreliable.
Sometimes we do not love God and neighbor
with all our heart.
We have a divided heart,
often loving false gods,
things not worthy of our heart.
God's love is perfect, however,
so we need not despair
as long as we begin each day
with the desire to love.

"As the Father has loved me, so I have loved you. . ."
(JOHN 15:9)

When we have our doubts
about God's love for us
all we need do
is look to the Jesus
of the Gospels.
We do not doubt that the Father
loves Jesus
therefore we cannot doubt that
Jesus loves us.
Repeat the words:
"Jesus loves me
with a never-ending love."
Repeat the words a few times.
Repeat the words
silently to yourself
whenever you think of it
throughout your day.
"Jesus loves me
with a never-ending love."
Soon, before you know it,

you will actually begin
to believe it.
Soon, before you know it,
you will begin to live
the truth of these words
from the inside out.
There is something wonderful,
you know,
about the life of a person
who believes these words
from the inside out.

For as the loincloth clings to one's loins, so I made
the whole house of Israel and the whole house of
Judah cling to me, says the LORD. . . (JEREMIAH 13:11)

Who says God does not smile?
Who says the Bible has no sense of humor?
Translate "loincloth" into modern terms,
and you get underpants.
Hilarity in the extreme.
You want to know how close I am to you? says
        the LORD.
I am as close to you as your underpants.
Ha! Knock yourself out laughing,
laughing with joy and relief.
God's loving presence is
as close as your Fruit of the Looms,
as close as your b.v.d.'s,
as close as your panties,
as close as your skivvies,
as close as your undies.
Laugh out loud,
tears streaming down your cheeks,
it is *soooo* funny!

God's love
is as close to you
as your underpants.
Fall down on the floor
laughing
with joy and gratitude,
that God would love you so,
so much that right there in the Bible
Jeremiah declares that God's love
clings to you like your unmentionables.
Think about that when you
get dressed in the morning.

Surely goodness and mercy shall follow me all the
days of my life, and I shall dwell in the house of the
LORD my whole life long.   (PSALM 23:6)

The Twenty-Third Psalm
is one of the best known
and most beloved
portions of Scripture.
Maybe this is so because
it reminds us of something
we so easily forget.
Much of the time we act as if
what follows us
all the days of our life
is not "goodness and kindness"
but something bleak and dark,
a God who stalks us
with an evil gleam in His eye,
a God who is out for revenge
and anxious to punish
for the slightest infraction of
the Rules.
Gonna get you for that,

and that, and that, and that. . .

But no, says Psalm Twenty-Three,
what follows you is
goodness and kindness,
and not just some of the time,
but all of the time.
All the days of your life.
Twenty-four hours a day,
goodness and kindness.
No matter how difficult times may be
what follows you is goodness and kindness.
Oh yes, believe it.

No one has greater love than this, to lay down one's life for one's friends. (JOHN 15:13)

The ultimate manifestation
of God's love for you
is the fact that
Jesus, the Son of God,
came into this world,
and embraced human existence
completely.
The Son of God
thought so highly of being
a human being
that he was identical to us
in all things except sin.
He was born of a human woman,
and he lived a human life,
teaching by word and example,
and he did not embrace just
the fun parts of being human,
the joy, the laughter, the ecstasy
of being human.

He embraced all that, of course.
But Jesus also accepted
the down side of being human.
He accepted the darkness,
and the fear,
and rejection by other people.
Jesus accepted death,
and not just an ordinary death
but the worst kind of death,
a death by torture and execution.
Jesus loves you more than he could say.
So he did it, instead.

Jesus. . .said to her, "Woman, where are they? Has no one condemned you?" She said, "No one, sir." And Jesus said, "Neither do I condemn you. Go your way, and from now on do not sin again." (JOHN 8:10-11)

You are a sinner,
you stinker you.
You make self-centered choices
devoid of love.
You sometimes make choices
that are self-destructive.
You sometimes make choices
that are bad for your
relationships with other people.
You sometimes make choices
that are bad for your relationship
with the earth, our home.
You sinner, you.
But God's love
does not and never will
condemn you.

In his whimsical, touching song,
"Interview With an Angel,"

singer/songwriter John Stewart
asks the angel if she has any advice.
"Yeah," the angel replies,
"Lose the mustache,
and try to be a little more nice."
This is the message of Jesus
in everyday, non-heroic terms:
Try to stop doing things that
make you look foolish,
and try to be a little nicer to
yourself, other people, and the earth.
You sinner, you.

For "In him we live and move and have our being";
as even some of your own poets have said, "For we
too are his offspring." (ACTS 17:28)

You might want to
be careful because
this one is dynamite.
Maybe leave it over there for a while,
watch it out of the corner of your eye
until it looks like everything is cool,
then sidle up to it nonchalantly.
"In him we live,
and move,
and have our being."
Holy hot tamale!
Where we live,
where we live all the time,
for crying out loud,
is in our God who is
nothing but love.
We can be no place else,
only in God's love.
You can be no place except
in God's love,

all the time and everywhere.

Relax, now.
Take a deep breath.
Breathe calmly in and out.
What you are breathing is
God's love for you,
in and out.
You are surrounded
and permeated by
God's love for you
all the live-long day.

Shower, O heavens, from above, and let the skies
rain down righteousness; let the earth open, that
salvation may spring up, and let it cause
righteousness to sprout up also; I the LORD have
created it. (ISAIAH 45:8)

God's love for you is steadfast.
God's love for you is unconditional.
God's love for you has no limit.
All you need to do is trust in that love.
In the words above from Isaiah
"righteousness" and "salvation"
mean basically the same thing.
They are equivalent to God's love
for you.
How does God's love come to you?
God's love comes to you as
spiritual healing and liberation.
God's love heals you
where it matters most.
God's love liberates you
in the ways you most need
to be liberated.

*H*ealing and freedom,
those are the effects of
God's love for you,
and God's love
showers down on you
from the heavens
like rain from the sky.
The earth opens up before you
and God's love springs up under your feet
like the flowers in the springtime.
Like rain and like flowers,
that is the way of God's love.

"Do not be afraid, little flock, for it is your Father's good pleasure to give you the kingdom." (LUKE 12:32)

In the Gospels, "the kingdom" is
a metaphor for God's all-embracing
love as it permeates the cosmos.
When Jesus admonishes his disciples
— which means us, too —
to not be afraid,
he does not say that we should
not be afraid
because God will save us
from all pain, anguish,
and hard times.
He says that we should not be afraid
because our Father
gives us His all-embracing,
all-penetrating love.

Jesus says that it is
our Father's "good pleasure"
to do this.
God takes pleasure
from giving us His love!

It's as if Jesus is saying
that we should not be afraid
because our Father loves us.
But then it's as if he is saying
that we need not worry
that our Father will stop
loving us,
because why would our Father
stop doing something
that He enjoys doing?
God's love is absolutely reliable.

". . .you are a gracious and merciful God. . . .the great and mighty and awesome God keeping covenant and steadfast love." (NEHEMIAH 9:31-32)

*J*esus just about knocked himself out,
as it were,
to teach us that God's love
is like the love of a strong
and kind and compassionate father
for his children.
"Abba" he called God,
"loving Papa."
Important as this is, however,
and straight from the lips of Jesus
as it is,
still it remains a metaphor,
and all metaphors,
as they say,
"limp."

*O*ur Father in heaven
loves us with an unconditional love.
But our God is greater than
any metaphor even Jesus used

to help us understand God's love.
Nehemiah reminds us that
our God is "great and mighty and awesome."
Of course, the two approaches
are certainly not mutually exclusive.
We might well blend the truth about
God's love for us
with the truth about
how great and mighty and awesome God is,
and then we have the truth that
God's love for us is
great and mighty and awesome.

Who will separate us from the love of Christ? Will hardship, or distress, or persecution, or famine, or nakedness, or peril, or sword?. . . No, in all these things we are more than conquerors through him who loved us. (ROMANS 8:35, 37)

We are so inclined
to believe
that God will stop loving us
for the slightest reason,
at the drop of a hat.
We are so inclined
to believe
that when pain,
or grief, or hard times
come to us
that must mean that
God does not love me.
But these things have
nothing to do
with God's love for us.
In fact, St. Paul declares,
even when the world lays us low,
when things look like

they couldn't get any worse,
"we are more than conquerors"
because we are loved by God.

There is, in short,
nothing to worry about
even when life is most worrisome.
Imagine the absolute worst.
Say you have been unjustly condemned.
As the firing squad takes aim,
there is nothing, nothing, nothing
to worry about.

Happy are you, O Israel! Who is like you, a people saved by the LORD, the shield of your help, and the sword of your triumph! (DEUTERONOMY 33:29)

We live in a peculiar world
when it comes to
religious attitudes.
Some people believe that
when you're saved, you're saved.
"Accept Jesus Christ as your
personal savior,"
and it's a done deal.
Others, however,
including Catholics,
believe that salvation
(spiritual healing and liberation)
is an ongoing process.
Instead of "saved"
we are "being saved."

Does this mean that God's love
is conditional?
That God doesn't love you completely
just yet?

Lord love a duck,
we should say not!
Rather, the lesson here
is that God's love is never static.
God is loving you all the time,
that is the point.
God is loving you, and loving you,
and loving you
all the time — even right now,
this very minute.
Be very quiet, very quiet.
God is loving you right now.

Book 2

Put things in order, listen to my appeal, agree with one another, live in peace; and the God of love and peace will be with you. (2 CORINTHIANS 13:11)

God loves you
with a love that overlooks
your faults and foibles
and forgives your offenses
the second you are sorry.
This is information
you can take to the bank.
At the same time,
there are connections
as far as the good God is concerned.
There are connections between
our relationship with God
and our relationships with
one another.
The more we live in peace
with one another
the more we will sense
God's loving presence with us.

Of course, the first place this truth
gathers meaning
is in our homes.
Family relationships
can be complicated and difficult,
as well as joyful and rewarding.
In both the joy and the anguish
of family relationships
we find connections to our
loving God.
Very often, we find God's love
in our love for one another.

As a deer longs for flowing streams, so my soul longs for you, O God. My soul thirsts for God, for the living God. (PSALM 42:1-2A)

The Great Commandment of Jesus
is to love God with our whole self
and our neighbor as our self.
Sometimes we hear that
the only way to love God
is to love our neighbor.
But this is not what Jesus
has in mind.
Clearly, we cannot love God
unless we love our neighbor, too.
But Jesus insists that we are to
love God directly.
The psalmist reminds us that
each of us has, deep inside,
an emptiness only God can fill.
The human heart longs for union
with God,
and this does not apply to mystics only.
Each and every one of us

longs for intimate, loving union
with God.

Sometimes we misinterpret our
hunger for God
and think it is hunger for something we can buy.
We think it is hunger for new furniture,
or hunger for a new car, or a can of beer,
or a new wardrobe, or another potato chip, or
        maybe
we interpret this hunger as simply
a vague dissatisfaction with life in general.
But what we hunger for more than anything
is personal, loving union with God.

But you are not in the flesh; you are in the Spirit,
since the Spirit of God dwells in you. (Romans 8:9a)

Here is how much God
loves you:
God loves you so much
that the Spirit of God
lives and breathes in you.
God loves you so much
that God's own Spirit
has taken up residence
in you.
You wonder where to find
God?
Look within,
look into your own
deepest center,
look into your own heart.

Sit quietly,
breathe evenly,
and ask God to
reveal Himself to you.
Ask God to

speak up in your life,
to help you know His love for you.
Pray this way:
"Loving God,
I love you.
Show yourself to me,
and help me to feel your love."
The Spirit of God dwells in you.
The Spirit of God
lives and breathes
and rejoices in you.

"Peace I leave with you; my peace I give to you. I do not give to you as the world gives. Do not let your hearts be troubled, and do not let them be afraid."

(JOHN 14:27)

Because God's love for us
is so great,
Jesus, the Son of God,
gives us his peace
for the asking.
But listen.
The peace that comes from the risen Christ
is not the kind of peace
we may have in mind.
For we may have in mind
the kind of peace that comes
from accumulating
financial forms of security,
and the approval of other people
for everything that we do,
and we tend to think we need
a lot more money and approval
than we really need.

No, the peace that comes
from the risen Christ
is a peace that does not depend
on circumstances,
financial or otherwise.
The peace that Christ gives
is a peace that stays with you
no matter how difficult life may become.
The peace that comes from
the risen Christ
is a deep-down peace
for the asking.

[Solomon] said, "O LORD, God of Israel, there is no God like you, in heaven or on earth, keeping covenant in steadfast love with your servants who walk before you with all their heart. . ."

(2 CHRONICLES 6:14)

*B*eyond doubt
and absolutely reliable,
that is the best description
of God's love
for you.
Of course,
our big problem
is believing this.
In our heads, maybe,
we believe it.
But along comes
the least little
threat to our security,
or some trouble,
and we give ourselves to the false gods
Fear and Anxiety.
We worship at their altars wholeheartedly,
bowing and bowing.

We need to make an effort
if we are to turn away from the false gods —
Fear and Anxiety —
to worship the true God
whose love is absolutely
trustworthy.
We need to make an effort
so weak is our faith.
But the least little effort
is all it takes,
and God's love is there
for you.

When the Lord saw her, he had compassion for her and said to her, "Do not weep." (LUKE 7:13)

We may view
all of the characters in the Gospels
as stand-ins
for us.
We need to believe this
because it is the gospel truth.
When Jesus feels compassion
for a woman whose son has died,
we need to understand
what this means for us.
This means that when you
experience pain or anguish
the risen Lord feels compassion
for you.
The love of God comes to you
just as it came to the woman
whose son had died.
Jesus gave the woman back
her son.

In one way or another
he will give you relief
from your pain and anguish.
The Lord Jesus speaks
to you
just as he spoke to
the bereaved woman.
He looks at you with compassion,
and says,
"Do not weep."
If you listen for his voice in your heart,
you will hear him speak.

*Grace to you and peace from God our Father and
the Lord Jesus Christ.* (1 Corinthians 1:3)

God's love comes to us
in many ways,
but they all add up to
"grace and peace."
Do you want to know
if God truly loves you?
Sit still and be quiet
for a few minutes.
Feel your heart
thumping in your chest.
Do you keep it going?
Do you will it to go on beating?
No.
The good God does that,
and it is the gift of grace and peace
for the taking.
Listen to your breathing,
in and out, in and out.
Do you breathe consciously
all the time, even when you are asleep?
No.

The gift of breath
is the gift of grace and peace,
and it is the gift of God's love for you.
God's love holds you in existence
from one moment to the next.
Do not doubt, therefore, that God loves you
because you have some
trouble in your life.
God's love holds you in existence,
the gift of grace and peace for the taking.

The Lord lives! Blessed be my rock, and exalted be
the God of my salvation. . . (Psalm 18:46)

There is no shortage of people
who say they "believe in God"
but live as if God is unreal,
irrelevant, meaningless,
or unimportant.
On the contrary, sings the psalmist.
"The Lord lives!"
Not only that, but the effect of
God's living, loving presence
is not difficult to identify.
"Salvation" is what we get
from God's love for us.
Trouble is, "salvation" is a word
that no longer lives up to
its reputation.
We no longer know what this word,
"salvation," means.

Here is what "salvation" means:
It means (are you ready for this?),
it means. . .LOVE,

God's love, to be specific.
God's healing and liberating love,
to be even more specific.
God's love as it heals and liberates you
from the inside out,
that's what "salvation" is.
God's love for a lifetime, every day,
that's what "salvation" is,
and it's your's, all your's,
in this world and the next.

"I give you a new commandment: love one another.
As I have loved you, so you also should love one
another." (JOHN 13:34) NAB

When Jesus gives us a new commandment,
that we are to "love one another,"
he takes his own love for us
for granted.
It goes without saying
that we can count on his love.
It goes without saying.
We have a tough time
believing this, however.
We can take God's love for us
for granted.

Don't even think of doubting
that God loves you.
Don't let it cross your mind,
and if it does cross your mind,
then remember the cross.
Jesus drank from the cup
of human existence,
and drained it to the last drop,

to the point of experiencing
a human death, even the worst kind
of human death.
He did this to show us his love.
So if it should cross your mind,
during a time of trouble or anguish,
to doubt God's love for you,
just remember the cross
where Jesus accepted the ultimate form
of human trouble,
in order to show us how to do it
with love.

For the one who sanctifies and those who are sanctified all have one Father. For this reason Jesus is not ashamed to call them brothers and sisters. . .

(HEBREWS 2:11)

*I*t boggles the mind
when you think about it.
Jesus, the Son of God,
insists that his Father is
our Father, too.
He does not say that God
is "kind of like" our Father, too.
Jesus says that God is
our Father
every bit as much as God is
his Father.

*D*oes God love you
with a never-ending love?
Will the sun rise
tomorrow morning?
The Father of Jesus
is our Father, too,
because Jesus makes us

his brothers and sisters.
Through the sacrament of Baptism
we become the sisters and brothers
of Jesus, the Son of God,
which makes us the sons and daughters
of God,
not just "so to speak,"
but in fact.
Does God love you,
His child?
Does a flower bloom
in the sunshine?

For in everything, O Lord, you have exalted and glorified your people, and you have not neglected to help them at all times and in all places.

(WISDOM 19:22)

Can we rely on God's love
to be there when we need it?
Is God's love reliable?
Not only is God's love
always there;
not only is God's love reliable;
but no matter where you are,
no matter what the circumstances,
no matter what the time,
God's love is always there,
closer than you are to yourself,
to support you
and give you strength;
to renew your hope
and renew your faith.
God's love "exalts and glorifies" you.

What does this mean?
It means that God's love,

for the asking,
helps you to stand up tall
when you would otherwise
bend over or fall down
from hopelessness or discouragement.
It means that God's love
fills your heart
for the asking
when you would otherwise
find in your heart
only a dark, dark emptiness.
God's love is always there for you.

*"But while he was still far off, his father saw him
and was filled with compassion; he ran and put his
arms around him and kissed him."* (Luke 15:20b)

To what can we compare
God's love for us?
There are all kinds of possibilities.
It is, how you say,
de rigeur these days
to observe that we can compare
God's love
to a mother's love.
Very true.
God's love is like
the love of a mother for her child.
But the Jesus of the Gospels,
for whatever reasons,
clearly prefers to present
God's love
as a father's love.

How does God love you?
Jesus tells the story of
the Prodigal Son,

whose father let him go
and make a fool of himself
when he chose to do so.
But when the son returned
the father ran to meet him,
and hugged and kissed him,
his heart filled with compassion.
How does God love you?
God loves you with a strong and reliable love,
a love that has no limits.

God is love, and those who abide in love abide in
God, and God abides in them. (1 JOHN 4:16B)

When the New Testament uses the word "love"
the Greek word translated there is *agapé*.
According to a theological dictionary, it means
"the selfless commitment of the lover
to the one loved,
to the enrichment and enhancement
of the beloved's being."
If God is *agapé*
that means that God is
selflessly committed
to us!
It means that God wants
above everything else
to enrich and enhance your being!

Of course,
God knows the ways
in which you need to be
enriched and enhanced,
and they may not be the ways
you think you need to be

enriched and enhanced.
God may not agree
that you most need to be enriched
by winning a lottery worth millions of clams.
God may not agree that
your life most needs to be enhanced
by freeing you, right now,
from all trouble and pain.
God's love for you means something
far better than that.

Let me sing for my beloved my love-song. . .

(ISAIAH 5:1)

Imagine the Lord God speaking to you
words of love.
Listen to those words,
for they are the truth of the matter.
Imagine the Lord God sings a
love song for you.
Can you imagine that?
Imagine it,
for that is the truth of the matter.
You are God's beloved.
That is the truth of the matter.
Do not doubt it,
even if you cannot
understand it.
You are God's beloved.
You are.

What does it mean to you
to know that God loves you
with an endless,
passionate love?

What does it mean to you
to know that God loves you
with a love that has no strings attached?
Does it make you feel like singing?
It should.
The Lord God sings a love song
to you.
So sing a love song in return.
The Lord God loves you,
Jesus declares,
like a loving Papa loves his children.
Don't you doubt it for a minute.

Do you not know that you are God's temple and that
God's Spirit dwells in you? (1 CORINTHIANS 2:16)

When we roll together
two or three insights from Scripture
and think about them at the same time,
sometimes they can blow your mind
— spiritually speaking, of course.
Think about this:
The First Letter of John tells us that
"God is love."
Now the First Letter of St. Paul to the Corinthians
reminds us that
"God's Spirit dwells in you."
So if we think about both of these truths
at the same time,
we must say that love
lives in you.
Not only does God love you,
but God,
who is love,
loves you so much
that He dwells in you.

Ponder this.
The infinite, eternal
creator of the universe,
and the Father of Jesus,
dwells in you.
Think about this long enough
and you are liable to faint from sheer joy.
Either that,
or you are liable to
start living a life based on
thankfulness and rejoicing.

Those who trust in [the LORD] will understand
truth, and the faithful will abide with him in love,
because grace and mercy are upon his holy ones, and
he watches over his elect. (WISDOM 3:9)

There is no need for worry,
and there is no need for anxiety,
for God watches over you
with love.
You are one of God's holy ones,
no matter what you may think
to the contrary.
You are one of God's holy ones
because, through Baptism,
you belong to the body of Christ.
God watches over you
with love.
God watches over you
with love.
Therefore,
grace and mercy
are upon you

at all times
and in all places.

*P*onder that
for a quick tinker's moment.
Grace and truth are upon you
at all times and in all places.
God watches over you with love,
and grace and mercy are upon you
right now, right here, and always.
Even if you are concerned about something,
push that worry far enough aside in your heart
so there is enough room for God's love
to squeeze in.
For God watches over you with love.

Great crowds came to him, bringing with them the lame, the maimed, the blind, the mute, and many others. They put them at his feet, and he cured them. . . (MATTHEW 15:30)

One can only imagine
the chaos of the crowds
bringing to Jesus
people with all kinds of afflictions.
"They put them at his feet,"
Matthew says,
"and he cured them."
That is all we need to know
about Jesus,
and that is all we need to know
about his love for
each one of us.
Matthew does not say
that Jesus cured only those
who suffered their affliction
in saintly silence.
Matthew does not say that
Jesus healed only those
who had great faith in him.

We may trust completely in
Jesus' love for us
knowing that we can expect
from his love
whatever kind of "cure" we need most.
Our "cure" may not be physical
because often that is not the kind of
cure that is most needed by everyone concerned.
Our cure may be of the spirit
which is the cure that matters most,
even when the cure is physical.

*Examine yourselves to see whether you are living in
the faith. Test yourselves. Do you not realize that
Jesus Christ is in you?* (2 CORINTHIANS 13:5)

Central to the meaning of "faith"
is the presence of the risen Christ "in you,"
that is, in the faith community.
But what exists in the community
exists in the individuals who
make up the community, as well.
So it is also true to say that
because you belong to
the community of faith,
therefore the risen Christ
is present in you
as an individual.
This is not to encourage
individualism, of course.
Rather, the point is to
remind yourself that
even when you are alone
you are never alone.

The risen Lord
who lives in the community
gathered together,
also lives in you,
no matter how alone you may feel.
The love of the risen Christ
fills your being,
and you are surrounded with
his grace and peace.
All you need do is acknowledge this
and be open to
the hope and joy that are yours.

*The LORD will make you the head, and not the tail;
you shall be only at the top, and not at the
bottom. . .* (DEUTERONOMY 28:13)

English poet Stevie Smith (1902-1971)
frequently said poetically and delightfully
what most of us keep to ourselves.
"What care I if good God be,"
she wrote,
"if he be not good to me?"
The title of the poem these words are from
is "Egocentric."
Which is just the point.
We tend to judge God
by our own self-centered standards.
"What care I if skies are blue,"
Stevie Smith asked,
"If God created Gnat and Gnu,
What care I if good God be
If he be not good to me?"

There is a great cosmic
scheme of things,

and much to our chagrin
we are not the center of it.
We cannot judge God's love
based merely on what happens
or does not happen
to me, myself, and I.
The long and the short of it is
that we cannot judge
by appearances.
You may be down,
but you are not out.
You may seem to be at the bottom,
when truly you are at the top.

While they were eating, he took a loaf of bread, and after blessing it he broke it, gave it to them, and said, "Take; this is my body." (MARK 14:22)

How can we doubt God's love
when we have the eucharist?
The faith community gathers together,
and the risen Jesus gives us
his whole self,
"body and blood, soul and divinity,"
to eat.
This is a great and deep mystery,
a great and deep mystery of love.
We receive to eat
the whole self of the risen Christ,
but what is "risen" body,
and what is "risen" blood?
We consume the mystery of our own
destiny,
which is resurrection in Christ.

What greater gift of love could there be?
When we celebrate the eucharist
the risen Lord is present in our midst,

and when we receive Communion
we receive his very risen self entire,
"body and blood, soul and divinity."
What greater gift of love
could there be?
If you find yourself in doubt
one day
about God's love for you,
take yourself to morning Mass
and let the love shine through,
let the love shine into you.
Let the love shine in you.

And I heard a voice from heaven saying, "Write this:
Blessed are the dead who from now on die in the
Lord." "Yes," says the Spirit, "they will rest from
their labors, for their deeds follow them."

(REVELATION 14:13)

Sometimes we harbor simpleminded ideas
about death
and about what happens after death.
Thomas Merton wrote (in *Learning to Love*):
"Instead of facing the inscrutable fact
that the dead are no longer there,
and that we don't know what happens to them,
we affirm that they are there, somewhere,
and we know. . .but we don't know,
and our act of faith should be less facile. . ."
Sometimes we may wonder about God's love
following the death of someone we love,
and it is natural that we should do so
because death is a question mark.
We can say with complete confidence
that we "die in the Lord."
But what does this mean?
We can say that those who "die in the Lord"

will "rest from their labors."
But what does this mean?

We have only words that lead us
deeper into the mystery.
We know that loved ones who have died
are loved by God unconditionally,
just as we ourselves
are loved by God unconditionally.
Therefore, whatever happens after death
is good beyond telling.
Whatever waits for us after death,
it is love eternal.

Gracious is the LORD, and righteous; our God is merciful. (PSALM 116:5)

Is there some trouble
in your life right now?
Is there some source of
anguish in your life
right now?
All God's children got trouble,
all God's children got anguish.
All God's children carry their crosses.
Pull that barge,
tote that bale,
carry that cross.
Not to make light of trouble
and anguish, of course.
Trouble and anguish are no fun.

All the same,
the most important thing
to remember
at times of pain and grief
is this, and this, and this:
"Gracious is the LORD,

and righteous;
our God is merciful."
Put your trust in God,
all your trust.
Which is to say,
put your trust in God's great love for you
and for all those you love.
Put your trust in the love
that keeps the earth
spinning through space
and keeps your heart thumping
in your chest.

[Jesus] took her by the hand and said to her,
"Talitha cum," which means, "Little girl, get up!"
And immediately the girl got up and began to walk
about (she was twelve years of age). (MARK 5:41-42A)

In the Gospels,
the overwhelming love of Jesus
for children
is never in doubt.
A twelve-year-old girl
seems to have died.
Jesus takes her by the hand
and says, "Little girl, get up!"
Whereupon the girl
sits up and bounces out of bed.
Jesus speaks these same words
to any child who may seem to be dead
in ways other than physical.
To the boy smoking cigarettes,
Jesus whispers and whispers in his heart,
"Little boy, wake up!"
To the teenager experimenting with drugs,
Jesus whispers and whispers,

"Wake up! Be free!"
To the girl abusing alcohol,
Jesus whispers and whispers,
"Be liberated! Be healed! Get up!"

We who are parents or teachers
are called to join the risen Christ
in prayer for children who are
dying or dead in one way or another.
We are called to join our love
to his love for children,
and we need have no doubt
about his love for them.

Grace to you and peace from God our Father and
the Lord Jesus Christ. (2 CORINTHIANS 1:2)

There is only one thing
that God gives,
regardless of appearances
and regardless of circumstances.
There is only one thing
that the Lord Jesus gives,
regardless of appearances
and regardless of circumstances.
This one thing is grace and peace.
Grace — which means that our Father gives
Himself to us
— is what God gives.
Peace — which means that our Father
is trustworthy
so we need not be anxious or afraid
— is what God gives to us.

Grace and peace,
grace and peace.
Because God our Father
loves you,

all you have at all times
is grace and peace.
The gift is already yours,
grace and peace are already
in your heart.
The challenge is to accept
what you already have
instead of living as if
you do not have it.
Grace and peace are yours.

The faithful will abound with blessings, but one who is in a hurry to be rich will not go unpunished.

(PROVERBS 28:20)

*O*h, my.
It's topsy-turvy time!
There simply is no end
to the blessings
that come from being faithful,
from living as if you can trust
in God's love for you,
which means you actually do trust
in God's love for you.
No end of blessings.

*M*any people, however, do not
believe God loves them.
It is much easier to believe in
the kind of security
money can buy,
so being wealthy is
a popular ideal.
Oh, to win a lottery
worth millions of clams!
We are in a hurry to be rich.

Trouble is,
the natural consequences
of hurrying to be rich
are invariably unpleasant.
Hurrying to be rich
means neglecting more important things.
Instead, we should hurry
to love God and neighbor
and then we shall be blessed,
and then we shall be free.

"This is my commandment, that you love one another as I have loved you."   (JOHN 15:12)

To know that you are loved
by the risen Christ,
loved in every atom of your being
can only lead to love
for other people.
Once you know that you are loved
you can't help but love others.
We have a problem
in our culture, of course,
with the word "love."
The Greek word translated as "love"
in the New Tesament is *agapé*.
It means unselfish concern for
and service to the other.
So the love of God moves us
to unselfish concern for
and service to others.

Nothing romantic about this.
In fact, we find ourselves
eyeball to eyeball

with the words of Dostoevsky's monk,
Zossima, in *The Brothers Karamazov.*
The kind, wise old monk declares that
"active love is a harsh and fearful thing
compared to love in dreams."
To love heroically — sooner or later
each and every one of us is called
to love heroically —
because we are loved unconditionally
by God our loving Father.

Blessed be the God and Father of our Lord Jesus
Christ, the Father of mercies and the God of all
consolation, who consoles us in all our affliction, so
that we may be able to console those who are in any
affliction with the consolation with which we
ourselves are consoled by God.　(2 CORINTHIANS 1:3-4)

If there is one thing we need
on a regular basis
it's "consolation."
The remarkable thing about
time spent in prayer
is that invariably
we come away from it
at least a little better off
than we were before.
Not talking about going from
the pits of depression
to the heights of ecstasy.
Talking about just
a little bit better.

In prayer we stand before
the God who loves us

no matter what,
"the Father of mercies
and the God of all consolation."
The monk Zossima, in Dostevsky's
The Brothers Karamazov, says that,
"Each time you pray,
if you do so sincerely,
there will be a flash of
a new feeling in it,
and a new thought as well. . .
which will give you fresh courage. . ."
After that, of course, it's time to share.

In the morning, while it was still very dark, [Jesus] got up and went out to a deserted place, and there he prayed. (MARK 1:35)

Where is God's love to be found?
Where can you go and be sure
that you will know that
God loves you,
and that God is trustworthy?
There is only one answer.
You will find that God loves you
in prayer.

If you find it difficult to pray,
perhaps because of some
anger or bitterness
or hopelessness in your heart,
then resolve to pray for five minutes only.
Let your five minutes of prayer
consist of just being present
and open to God.
There is no need to say anything.
Or, if you feel like talking to God,
then remember that you are talking

to your Father in heaven in your deepest center,
and tell Him how you are feeling
honestly.
Tell your heavenly Father
about your anger or anxiety
or hopelessness.
Pour out your heart to God,
and then just be present and open
to whatever response you may get,
even if it seems to be nothing.
Soon, before very long,
you will know God's love for you.

For you know the generous act of our Lord Jesus Christ, that though he was rich, yet for your sakes he became poor, so that by his poverty you might become rich. (2 CORINTHIANS 8:9)

Another way to look at
God's unconditional love
for you
is to see that you are
fabulously wealthy
in a way
no lottery can ever make you.
We live in a culture,
of course,
that constantly pushes you
to be dissatisfied
with what you already have,
materially speaking,
a culture that knows little,
if anything, about
personal and spiritual values.
Therefore, just about everybody
feels dissatisfied, discontented,
and restless.

Instead, be at peace,
for chances are you have
more than you need.
Indeed, you have everything
if you know that God
your loving Father
holds you in His heart
at all times
and in all places,
no matter what your circumstances,
no matter what your situation.

Book 3

. . .I am the LORD; I act with steadfast love, justice, and righteousness in the earth, for in these things I delight, says the LORD. (JEREMIAH 9:24)

There is no end of
surprises from our God,
the main surprise being
that our God is a God of
steadfast love,
a love that will not change
with the shifting winds of
fashion, or
circumstances.
People are fickle,
our God is not.
Steadfast love is the
bottom line,
no matter what else
is percolating in the pot.

G. K. Chesterton,
that joyful genius,
once said:
"Let your religion be

less of a theory and
more of a love affair."
There you go.
That's what God has with you,
you know,
a love affair.
You are no theory to God,
so don't let God be a theory
for you.
Instead,
abandon yourself to
the love affair.

And [Jesus] said to the woman, "Your faith has saved you; go in peace." (LUKE 7:50)

What do you think Jesus
says to you?
Do you think he says,
"You hard-hearted sinner,
away with you,
I despise you"?
Sometimes we act as if
that is what Jesus says
to us.
We silently whine
and beg
and grovel
and whimper
when all along the risen Lord
repeats over and over
in our heart
— if only we would listen:
"Your faith has saved you;
go in peace."

The trouble is
that this is so difficult to accept.
We find it tough to believe
that Jesus would be so forgiving
and compassionate
and understanding,
and would say, just like that,
"Your faith has saved you;
go in peace."
End of discussion.
But that is exactly what he says
to you.

. . .God's love has been poured into our hearts
through the Holy Spirit that has been given to us.

(ROMANS 5:5)

Sometimes it takes a poet
to awaken in us,
once again,
an appreciation for what it means
to say that God loves us.
Mark Van Doren wrote a poem
called "He Loves Me"
that pulls it off beautifully.
"That God should love me is more wonderful
Than that I so imperfectly love him. . ."
Van Doren wrote.

"But when he looks he loves me. . ."
That's all it takes, you know.
God takes one look at you
and falls head over heels in love
with you,
and it happens every moment
of every day.
Even while you sleep

God looks at you and
can't help Himself.
God takes one look at you
and loves you,
couldn't care less about
what you see as imperfections,
idiosyncracies, and sins.
Couldn't care less,
so deeply does God love you,
so deeply does the Lord of the universe
love you.
Head over heels in love.

Let your steadfast love, O LORD, be upon us, even as we hope in you. (PSALM 33:22)

There is a famous story
about St. Teresa of Avila.
As she traveled the hard, dusty roads
of sixteenth-century Spain,
Teresa had more than her share
of anguish and hard times.
So she remarked wryly to the Lord, one time,
that if this was how He treated His friends
it was no wonder He didn't have more of them.
The lesson for us, of course,
is that the presence of hard times
and anguish in our lives
does not mean
that God does not love us.
After all, Jesus certainly had
more than his share of
pain and suffering.

There is something mysterious
about life, something we can't quite

put our finger on.
Perhaps St. Paul got close to it
when he remarked that
"the whole creation has been groaning
in labor pains until now;
and not only the creation,
but we ourselves,
who have the first fruits of the Spirit,
groan inwardly while we wait for adoption,
the redemption of our bodies."
God's love comes to us
even in the midst of anguish and hard times.

"And remember, I am with you always, to the end of the age." (MATTHEW 28:20B)

Sometimes we feel so alone.
Indeed, loneliness is frequently identified
as a characteristic of our time.
"All the lonely people,"
sang the Beatles way back when,
"where do they all come from?"
But a faith that is grown up,
that has paid its dues,
understands that, truly,
there is no need to be lonely.
Hubert Van Zeller, an English Benedictine monk
and popular spiritual writer
during the 1950s,
explained the situation well.
"The soul hardly ever realises it,
but whether he is a believer or not,
his loneliness is really
a homesickness for God."

When we are alone, feeling lonely,

that is the time to recall that
the risen Lord
is with us always,
as much when we are alone
as when we are with others.
Indeed, sometimes we are more alone
in the company of other people
than we are when we are alone.
Feeling lonely
is nothing but a reminder
to recall God's deep love for us.

May mercy, peace, and love be yours in abundance.

This is our inheritance,
you know:
"mercy, peace, and love. . .in abundance."
As children of God
and brothers and sisters of Christ
by adoption through Baptism,
we receive mercy, peace, and love
in abundance.
This is our condition
here and now,
now and here:
mercy-laden,
filled with peace,
and loved by God
with an unconditional, infinite love.
This is where we are,
and this is who we are.

Pause.
Close your eyes.
Breathe deeply and evenly, calmly.

You are loved completely, totally,
and there is no need to be afraid
of what the future may bring.
You are loved unconditionally,
and there is no need to surrender to
anxiety or worry.
Close your eyes.
Breathe in God's love for you.
Breathe out the poison of fear
and anxiety.
Let God's love settle deeply
into your heart and into your bones.

God saw everything that he had made, and indeed, it was very good.   (GENESIS 1:31)

Sometimes we overlook
the most obvious signs of
God's love for us.
Watch the world pass from
the dead of winter
into the rebirth and new life
of spring.
That's God telling us
what life is about
and what happens to us
when we die, as well.

When we watch a beautiful sunset,
or gaze at the ocean,
or marvel at the delicate beauty
of a tiny wildflower,
we get a message about
God's love for us.
When we get ourselves out
into a place where
the artificial lights of civilization

are not present,
where we can really see
the star-filled night sky,
we get a message about
God's uninhibited love for us.
When we enjoy a good meal,
or drink sweet, fresh, pure water
untainted by chemicals or pollution,
we get a message about God's love
for us.
God's gifts of love are all around us.

Jesus said to them, "I am the bread of life. Whoever comes to me will never be hungry, and whoever believes in me will never be thirsty." (JOHN 6:35)

There is food,
and there is food.
There is bread,
and there is bread.
We need the food
that keeps us physically alive,
and it is sacred.
We need the bread
that gives nourishment
to our bodies,
and it is sacred bread.
But in the long run
and all along the way
we need the bread of eternal life,
which is Jesus the Lord.
We receive the risen Christ
when we receive Holy Communion.

But the Lord Jesus who is
the bread of life

and the ultimate gift of God's love
for us,
comes to us in every moment of the day
and every breath we breathe.
To go to him
is to be fed on God's love.
To turn to him in our heart
is to be nourished by God's love
which means the end of ultimate hunger
and the end of ultimate thirst.
To welcome the Lord Jesus into your heart
is to be one with God's love for you.

. . .agree with one another, live in peace; and the God of love and peace will be with you.

(2 Corinthians 13:11)

On the one hand,
it is true that God loves us
with an unconditional love.
On the other hand, it is also true
that our Father wants us to
live in peace with one another.
Sometimes it seems like
God will love us only if we
love one another.
That would be a heavy trip,
would it not?

The truth is more like this:
If we truly believe,
if we truly feel
and experience
God's unconditional love,
we will,
as the night follows the day,
love one another

and live in peace with one another.
God's love and peace
lead to love and peace
between people,
or at least the desire
to be at peace
with one another.
You want a parish community
filled with love and peace?
Help people to experience God's love
and you will have the parish community
you want.

For we are slaves; yet our God has not forsaken us
in our slavery, but has extended to us his steadfast
love. . . (EZRA 9:9)

We hear a good deal these days
about addictions of various sorts.
Addictions seem widespread,
common even.
Addiction to everything from nicotine
to alcohol,
from caffeine to cocaine,
from sex to candy bars.
But what is an addiction if not
a form of psychological, emotional,
even spiritual slavery?
Difficult to say to what extent
human freedom is involved
when it comes to addictions.
Regardless, God does not abandon us
in our addictions.

Our Father in heaven (right here)
does not give up on us
even if we give up on ourselves.

Instead, God doubles His efforts
to fill us, surround us, gift us
with His steadfast love.
Indeed, one of our greatest sources of
strength
in the face of an addiction
is the knowledge that God's love
is more powerful than any addiction.
We need never lose hope
because God's love is there for us,
closer to you than you are to yourself.
Always.

Jesus answered, "The first [commandment] is, 'Hear, O Israel: the Lord our God, the Lord is one; you shall love the Lord your God with all your heart, and with all your soul, and with all your mind, and with all your strength.'" (MARK 12:29-30)

When we realize
the endless depth
of God's love for us,
it touches us deeply.
We are filled with joy,
and life takes on new meaning.
But how often do we reflect on
our need to love God in return?
God does not need our love,
but we need to love God
if we are to be all that we can be.
If we do not love God
we find ourselves loving
something less than God.
Call it the worship of a
false god.
If we do not love God

we will shrivel
from the inside out.

How to love God
when God seems absent?
Sit still, breathe evenly, calmly,
open yourself,
and ask God to show you His love.
Before long you will feel God's love
for you,
and you will only be able to love God
in return,
with gratitude, with thanksgiving.

"What no eye has seen, nor ear heard, nor the human heart conceived, what God has prepared for those who love him." (1 CORINTHIANS 2:9)

What it all comes down to
is this:
God's love is so complete,
so worthy of our trust
that even when only the worst
outcome seems possible,
even then the ultimate outcome
is bound to be better than
we could ever imagine.
Can you imagine a love
and a joy
that is beyond imagining?
Of course not.
But just the thought of a
love and a joy
that is greater than any
we could ever imagine
is a thought filled with
great comfort and encouragement.

Sometimes we may actually feel guilty
about wanting to be comforted
by our God.
We may think that
we do not deserve comfort.
Yes, God challenges us to grow
and beckons us to love one another.
But St. Paul reminds us that
at the end of our journey
and all along the way, as well,
there waits for us a joy and a love
beyond imagining.

When you come into the land that the LORD your
God is giving you, you must not learn to imitate the
abhorrent practices of those nations.

(DEUTERONOMY 18:9)

Through our baptism into
the death and resurrection of Christ
we have come into,
and are on our way into,
the Promised Land,
the kingdom of God.
We are already there,
but we are not completely there yet.
We enjoy God's saving love,
but we are still moving on down the line,
and along the way, sometimes,
we discover that we are
strangers in a strange land.
We find ourselves face-to-face
with ideas, and values, and ways of thinking
that clash with the
ideas, and values, and ways of thinking
that come with the kingdom of God.

One of the gifts of God's love
is the power to recognize
ideas, and values, and ways of thinking
that lead not to life
but to death.
God's love enables us to turn aside
from death
and seek life at every turn.
God's love enables us to live in Christ,
who is "the way, the truth, and the life."

*[Jesus said to Peter,] "Go to the sea and cast a hook;
take the first fish that comes up; and when you open
its mouth, you will find a coin; take that and give it
to them for you and me."*   (MATTHEW 17:27)

There is something so charming,
and so mysterious,
and delightful
about the little anecdote in Matthew's Gospel
where Jesus tells Peter to
pluck a coin from the mouth of a
just-caught fish
in order to pay the temple tax
for the two of them.
Matthew does not tell us
if Peter actually did this or not,
but we may assume that he did.
In a way, this story is a metaphor
for what Christ does
for each one of us.

From out of nowhere, it seems,
God's love appears
for each one of us

when we need it most.
The love of God saves us
in the most unlikely ways sometimes.
In mysterious, delightful ways,
God's love saves us
and keeps us on track
when we need it the most
and expect it the least.
It's as if Jesus says
to each one of us
to go pluck our salvation
from the mouth of a fish.

But God, who is rich in mercy, out of the great love
with which he loved us even when we were dead
through our trespasses, made us alive together with
Christ. . .and raised us up with him and seated us
with him in the heavenly places in Christ Jesus. . .

(EPHESIANS 2:4-6)

No matter how many times
we remind ourselves that
God loves us with an endless love,
sometimes we still find it difficult
to believe,
that God could love us.
St. Paul patiently explains, however,
that God loves us so much
that He identifies us with Christ,
so that his destiny is our destiny, as well.

In other words, God loves us so much
that He gives us a full share in
the resurrection of Christ,
which means that our eternal destiny
is the same as that of the Lord Jesus.
We are destined to be

"seated. . .in the heavenly places
in Christ Jesus."
This has already been decided,
Paul says;
it has already been accomplished,
there is no question about it.
Our God is "rich in mercy,"
and that is all we need to know,
that is all we need to keep in mind
when we find ourselves
wondering or worrying
about the future,
near or far.

But you are a God ready to forgive, gracious and
merciful, slow to anger and abounding in steadfast
love. . .   (NEHEMIAH 9:17)

Nobody denies
that we regularly make a mess of things.
Nobody denies that
we are sometimes selfish,
mean-spirited, impatient,
and unforgiving.
Nobody denies that we
frequently act as if we have no faith.
Nobody denies that
we find it difficult to trust in God.
Nobody denies that when it comes to
faith, hope, and love,
we are sometimes
faithless, hopeless, and loveless.

What we need to keep in mind
is that even though all this,
and much more of a negative nature,
is true,
all the same what's more important
is that our God is

"ready to forgive,
gracious and merciful
. . .abounding in steadfast love."
In the long run and the short run,
this is all that matters.
Our God is "abounding in steadfast love."
For you, even, God is
abounding in steadfast love.
For you, even, you there,
not one of the great sinners of all time,
God's steadfast love is abounding.

And [Jesus] answered them, "Go and tell John what you have seen and heard: the blind receive their sight, the lame walk, the lepers are cleansed, the deaf hear, the dead are raised, the poor have good news brought to them." (LUKE 7:22)

If we had to sum up
the meaning and message
of Jesus
in a few words,
it would come to something
like this:
In Jesus, God's love becomes
visible in the world
for all to see.
Jesus is God's love
made visible,
and what we see Jesus doing
in the Gospels
we see him doing
in our own time and place
and in our own life.

When we accept God's love

and are open to that love
we find ourselves being
healed, liberated, re-born.
We find ourselves
with a new life to live.
This is what God's love
brings:
a new life to live,
a life centered not on self
but a life centered on
love for God and neighbor.
It's as simple and glorious as that.

To him who loves us and freed us from our sins by his blood, and made us to be a kingdom, priests serving his God and Father, to him be glory and dominion forever and ever. Amen. (REVELATION 1:5B-6)

The entire Gospel,
in a nutshell,
is the simple message
that we are loved by our God
who created us
and holds us in being
from one moment
to the next.
The One who created us
also loves us.
God loves each person
as if he or she
were the only human being
in existence.
God our Father loves you
far more than any human father
ever loved his child.

At the same time,

if you would like a hint
of how
and how much
God loves you,
keep your eye on
a father sometime
who obviously loves
his child.
Watch closely,
and you will get some
vague idea
of how much God loves you.

But you, our God, are kind and true, patient, and
ruling all things in mercy.　　　(WISDOM 15:1)

Why are we more inclined
to think of God as angry and punishing
than we are inclined
to think of God as
loving and merciful?
Maybe because we ourselves
are more inclined to be
angry and punishing?
But our God is better than us,
and our ways are not God's ways.
How many times
do we need to hear
the First Letter of John declare that
"God is love"
before we will be ready to
believe it?

Our God is above all
merciful,
"Mercy within mercy within mercy,"

wrote Thomas Merton.
Our God is above all
kind and
true and
patient.
With us — with you,
not the greatest sinner
of all time
  — God is above all kind,
and true,
and patient.
Above all, kind and patient.

"I am the good shepherd. I know my own and my own know me, just as the Father knows me and I know the Father. And I lay down my life for the sheep." (JOHN 10:14-15)

In Jesus we find
the fullest manifestation of God
that is possible
for the human mind to grasp.
Jesus shows us
what God is like
precisely by being human.
He then tells us what his love
for us is like.
Jesus uses the metaphor of
a good shepherd,
and says that
in his relationship with us
that is what we should expect.
We should expect him
to care for us
and protect us
like a good shepherd
cares for the sheep.

*T*he point is not that we are sheep.
The point is that the risen Lord
cares for us like a shepherd
cares for the sheep.
He cares for you
to the point of
giving his life for you.
Just as a good shepherd
may give his life to save the sheep,
so the Lord Jesus gives his life
out of love for us.

"Come to me, all you that are weary and are
carrying heavy burdens, and I will give you rest.
Take my yoke upon you, and learn from me; for I am
gentle and humble in heart, and you will find rest for
your souls. For my yoke is easy, and my burden is
light."   (MATTHEW 11:28-30)

*I*nspired Matthew,
putting together his Gospel for
a predominantly Jewish Christian audience,
meant these words of Jesus to apply,
first of all,
to the heavy burden
of a legalistic observance
of the Jewish law.
In spite of what we are inclined to think,
Jesus is not saying that
he will carry the heavy burdens of life
for you.
He does not say that
he will take your suffering
and your anguish
on his shoulders
if you rely on him.

*H*e says that if you
take his yoke — the "yoke" of
Christian discipleship —
on your shoulders
you will find it a light burden,
compared to a life
based on legalistic observances
of any kind.
Of course, at the same time,
if you ask the risen Lord
to help you carry your various crosses,
he will do that, too.

The compassion of human beings is for their
neighbors, but the compassion of the Lord is for
every living thing. . .He has compassion on those
who accept his discipline and who are eager for his
precepts. (SIRACH 18:13-14)

Do not worry the night away
asking if God loves you.
Do you care for those closest to you?
Do you?
Of course.
Just so God loves you
but with a love that has no limits,
a love that encompasses
every living thing,
and even things that do not seem
to be alive:
God loves rocks,
for example,
and minerals
in the earth.

God loves all things,
and God loves you

as if you were the only thing
worth loving.
God loves you
from the inside out
and from the outside in.
God's love permeates every cell
of your being.
God's love is even
in the spaces between your cells.
God's love
is in the spaces between the
atoms that make up your physical self.

When the steward tasted the water that had become
wine, and did not know where it came from. . .the
steward called the bridegroom and said to him,
"Everyone serves the good wine first, and then the
inferior wine after the guests have become drunk.
But you have kept the good wine until now."

(JOHN 2:9-10)

Here is how God's love works
very often in our lives:
it comes into your life
and turns something ordinary
into something extraordinary.
Just when you thought
you were stuck with
a bad situation
it turns out to be a blessing.
Or, just when you thought there was
no hope,
something happens,
and the situation does not look
so hopeless after all.

You might say that

life is like a baseball game.
Sometimes, when the count is
three and two,
you give it one more try
and, by golly,
you single to right field.
You just never know
when that is going to happen,
in baseball or in life.
God's love is like that,
frequently turning
something ordinary or hopeless
into something special or promising.

When I saw him, I fell at his feet as though dead.
But he placed his right hand on me, saying, "Do not
be afraid; I am the first and the last, and the living
one. I was dead, and see, I am alive forever and
ever. . ." (Revelation 1:17-18)

Times come along,
sometimes,
when we don't know if we can
face another day.
Hard times, painful times,
times of anguish and sadness.
At such times
we can turn to the risen Lord
who lives in us
and ask for his support.
At such times
his words to us are
few and simple.
They go like this:
"Do not be afraid."

He does not deny the reality of
your anguish, or pain, or sorrow.

He does not ask you to pretend
that it isn't there.
He simply says that
whatever makes you sad or
gives you pain
is nothing to be afraid of.
He says this because
in the long run and the short run
his love covers all and saves all.
Eternal life and eternal joy
are the beginning and end of the story
for all of us.

And the LORD restored the fortunes of Job when he
had prayed for his friends; and the LORD gave Job
twice as much as he had before. (JOB 42:10)

Nobody knows the troubles I've had,
moans Job,
and his story goes on at length,
for forty-two, count 'em, forty-two, chapters.
The story of Job is the classic example
of someone who has grief and misery
on top of grief and misery.
When Job complains,
God replies with the classic comeuppance.
He advises Job to clam up
because God is infinitely wiser than Job,
and He knows what He is doing.
"Where were you
 when I laid the foundation of the earth?
Tell me, if you have understanding. . . .
On what were its bases sunk,
or who laid its cornerstone
when the morning stars sang together
and all the heavenly beings shouted for joy?"

Hush up, Job, you whiner, God says.

Sometimes this is the form God's love takes,
the dawning realization that
even when life looks darkest
our best move is to trust.
And when do things improve for Job?
They improve after Job prays not for himself
but for his friends.
Miserable as he is,
Job manages to forget his own woes
long enough to pray for his friends.

And [the angel Gabriel] came to [Mary] and said,
"Greetings, favored one! The Lord is with you."

(Luke 1:28)

When the angel Gabriel speaks to Mary
he calls her "favored one."
Ever after that,
we can think of ourselves
in the same way.
Because you are baptized
into Christ,
a member of his body,
the Church,
you also are God's "favored one."
Because you are in Christ,
"The Lord is with you," too.

There is no doubt that God loves you
and cherishes you
as His own child.
God holds you
in the palm of His hand,
caring for you,
watching over you,

no matter what else
may seem to be going on
in your life.
In difficult times
turn to God for comfort,
and you will receive it.
When you need courage
ask for it;
act as if you had it,
and courage will be given to you.
Wherever you go
angels go with you. . .

May grace and peace be yours in abundance in the knowledge of God and of Jesus our Lord. His divine power has given us everything needed for life and godliness, through the knowledge of him who called us by his own glory and goodness. (2 PETER 1:2-3)

We have such a difficult time
believing the good news.
So beaten down are we
by the daily grind
that we forget the daily blessing.
So close do we keep
our nose to the grindstone
that we do not see
God's love all around us.
So clouded is our vision
by the activities
of everyday life
that we miss signs of God's love
in the people
we meet each day.
When things do not go
the way we want them to go

we whine and feel sorry for ourselves.
We overlook the reality of God's love
glowing in our deepest center.

God's grace and peace
are yours in abundance,
but how often do you
allow yourself
to feel that grace and peace?
How often do you pause,
breathe deeply and calmly,
and allow God's grace and peace
to well up in your heart?

The beloved of the LORD rests in safety — the High God surrounds him all day long — the beloved rests between his shoulders. (DEUTERONOMY 33:12)

Sometimes it seems as if the Scriptures
drone on almost endlessly
about God's steadfast love.
You are God's beloved,
therefore you "rest in safety."
You are God's beloved,
therefore God "surrounds" you
"all day long,"
and all night long, too.
God is so close to you
that Deuteronomy even says that
you "rest between his shoulders."

Resting between God's shoulders!
It is amazing and delightful!
Imagine God's shoulders,
if you can.
Well, why not?
The strong, broad shoulders

of a loving Papa,
the Father of Jesus
and our Father, too.
There you are,
resting between God's shoulders.
Every minute of the day,
when you begin to feel anxious
or afraid, or worried, or
you find it hard to trust in
God's love for
someone you love,
think of yourself resting
between God's shoulders.

"Which one of you, having a hundred sheep and losing one of them, does not leave the ninety-nine in the wilderness and go after the one that is lost until he finds it? When he has found it, he lays it on his shoulders and rejoices." (LUKE 15:4-5)

Jesus has it all wrong
if he thinks we, today,
will, say, leave a large crowd of folks
who need our help
to go off and search for
a single lost soul who also needs our help
and has wandered off someplace.
That's not how we work.
That turkey wants to wander away
and get lost,
we're not about to leave
all these other folks
who need our attention.

But that's just the point.
Our Father in heaven
does not act like we do.
You wander off,

literally or figuratively,
and you can bet your last buffalo nickel
He is on your trail right now,
searching for you,
calling your name in the darkness,
looking for you,
hoping you will come home
sooner rather than later.
Notice that image of "shoulders" again.
The minute you let God find you
up you go on His shoulders,
and what you hear is God rejoicing.

If God is for us, who is against us?   (ROMANS 8:31B)

*U*ltimately,
this is what it comes down to.
Nothing is greater
or more powerful
than God's love for you.
Nothing is more trustworthy
than God's love for you.
Nothing is more reliable
than God's love for you.
You think times are tough?
You think the darkness is going to win?
Does it look like the night will never end?
God's love is there for you
even in the face of certain death,
and death has no power over God's love.

*T*he steadfast love of God
is always there
ready to fill your heart
at the slightest invitation.
All you need do is ask,
invite God to come into your heart,

and you will find that
no matter how bleak
prospects seem to be,
time will bring you out
on the other side of the darkness
into God's wonderful light.
The point is not that
God saves us from all
anguish and pain.
The point is that God's love is victorious.

*But you, O LORD, are a shield around me, my glory,
and the one who lifts up my head.* (PSALM 3:3)

St. Thomas Aquinas wrote
in his *Summa Theologiae*:
"Mercy starts all God's works
and grows in all that follows,
God always giving
beyond the measure
of a creature's due."
The essence of God's love
for you
is mercy.
So give up thinking
that God does not love you
very much
because you do not deserve to be loved.
It is true that you do not deserve
God's love,
but it is also irrelevant.
God's mercy
is all that is relevant.

One glance at you,
and God can't help Himself.
He loves you with a love
that goes beyond reason.
You stand there
with your face hanging out,
and God can't help but love you.
God loves you helplessly,
as it were.
All that is required of you
is to accept God's love.
So give in and accept.

From his fullness we have all received, grace upon grace. (JOHN 1:16)

God loves you,
and loves you,
and loves you
endlessly.
That is the beginning
and the end
of the truth
about your existence.
God's love keeps you,
from one moment to the next,
from vanishing,
with a little pop,
into nothingness.

Do you want physical proof
that God loves you?
Hold your hand over your heart
and feel it thumping in your chest.
Do you keep your heart beating
by an act of your own will?
Your heart just goes on thumping away,

and this is as close as you will get
to physical proof that God loves you.
There is no other explanation, ultimately,
for why your heart goes on beating out
the rhythm of your life.
God does it, keeps your heart beating out
the rhythm of your life.
And when your physical life
comes to its natural end
a great light fills your being,
and the light is God's love for you
that was there all your life long.

A Final Thought. . .

St. Irenaeus (c. 125 – c. 203), one of the earliest Fathers of the Church, whistled up something basic to the Christian life. He said:

God did not make the first human because He needed company, but because He wanted someone to whom he could show His generosity and love. God did not tell us to follow Him because He needed our help, but because He knew that loving Him would make us whole.

This, of course, is what this collection of meditations is all about — God's infinite love for us and our need to love God in return. As many times as this truth is repeated in this book, it bears repeating endlessly. Listen: God's steadfast love for you is beyond doubt. Absolutely. Keep this truth in your pocket like a coin. Cultivate it in your heart like a flower. Never let it out of your sight. Never.

Finally, gentle reader, a blessing in the words of singer/song writer John Stewart: "May the songs of all the angels sing within your soul."

Amen, and again Amen.

Published by Resurrection Press

For a free catalog call 1-800-892-6657